STORIES OF
HONOR

Published in the United States of America by Cherry Lake Publishing
Ann Arbor, Michigan
www.cherrylakepublishing.com

Content Adviser: Satta Sarmah Hightower, www.sattasarmah.com
Reading Adviser: Marla Conn MS, Ed., Literacy specialist, Read-Ability, Inc.

Photo Credits: ©Inti St Clair/Thinkstock Images, cover, 1; ©michaeljung/Shutterstock Images, 5; ©Anthony22/
Wikimedia, 7; ©Henry Alexander Ogden/Wikimedia, 8; ©Wikimedia, 11; ©Bernard Spragg/Wikimedia, 12;
©Nadezda Murmakova/Shutterstock Images, 15; ©Meiqianbao/Shutterstock Images, 16; ©DR Travel Photo and
Video/Shutterstock Images, 17; ©Erofeenkov/Shutterstock Images, 18; ©Sergey Uryadnikov/Shutterstock Images, 21;
©360b/Shutterstock Images, 22; ©PD-US/Steve Petteway/Wikimedia, 25; ©Obama White House/Flickr, 26;
©Billion Photos/Shutterstock Images, 28

Library of Congress Cataloging-in-Publication Data
Names: Colby, Jennifer, 1971- author.
Title: Stories of honor / by Jennifer Colby.
Description: Ann Arbor : Cherry Lake Publishing, [2018] | Series: Social emotional library |
    Audience: Grade 4 to 6. | Includes bibliographical references and index.
Identifiers: LCCN 2017035924 | ISBN 9781534107465 (hardcover) | ISBN 9781534109445 (pdf) |
    ISBN 9781534108455 (pbk.) | ISBN 9781534120433 (hosted ebook)
Subjects: LCSH: Honor—Biography—Juvenile literature.
Classification: LCC BJ1533.H8 C65 2018 | DDC 177—dc23
LC record available at https://lccn.loc.gov/2017035924

Cherry Lake Publishing would like to acknowledge the work of The Partnership for 21st Century Learning.
Please visit www.p21.org for more information.

Printed in the United States of America
Corporate Graphics

ABOUT THE AUTHOR

Jennifer Colby is a school librarian in Michigan. She honors others by listening
to them and trying to understand their points of view.

TABLE OF CONTENTS

What Is Honor?

Do you show respect to anyone in your life? If you do, then you honor them. We honor people for many different reasons— for their age, for their relationship to us, or for their rank in their career. We also honor people for their knowledge, their experience, or their actions. Have you ever made a promise? Maybe you told your parents you would finish your homework every night without being asked. If you did it, then you are honorable. You are considered honorable when you follow through on promises you make. Many honorable people throughout time have earned our respect for what they have accomplished.

Awarding someone for their work is another way of honoring them.

CHAPTER 2

Sybil Ludington

If your father asked you to go on a dangerous mission, would you do it? That is exactly what Sybil Ludington did during the American Revolution. She was one of many riders who traveled through the New England countryside during the war to warn people of British attacks. Best known is Paul Revere, whose ride was made famous by the poem called "Paul Revere's Ride" by Henry Wadsworth Longfellow. Ludington is honored for being the youngest rider and the only female to make such a difficult journey.

Born April 5, 1761, in Fredericksburg (now named Ludingtonville), New York, Sybil Ludington was the oldest of Colonel Henry Ludington and his wife Abigail's 12 children. Sybil and her sister Rebecca were often in charge of the family's

Ludington owned a horse named Star.

safety when their father was away. On the night of April 26, 1777, Colonel Ludington—an assistant to General George Washington— was warned that British troops were going to attack Danbury, Connecticut. He was needed for battle, but he needed a messenger. Colonel Ludington and his troops of the 7th **Regiment** of the Dutchess County **Militia** in New York State were scattered around the county. He ordered 16-year-old Sybil to ride through the countryside to warn his men to gather at the family's home. She accepted the job with honor, aware that there was no one else who could fulfill the duty.

The soldiers in the Continental Army wore blue uniforms.

Known for her horsemanship, Sybil rode 40 miles (64 kilometers) through the night and returned by dawn, exhausted and wet from the rain. She rode more than twice as far as Paul Revere. Impressively, she managed to gather her father's 400 men while evading advancing British troops. Unfortunately, Colonel Ludington's regiment did not arrive in time to protect Danbury. Instead, the regiment battled the British troops as they left the burning city. Sybil continued to assist her father as a messenger during the remainder of the war. After it ended, she married an innkeeper and had one son. In 1839, she died at the age of 77.

[21ST CENTURY SKILLS LIBRARY]

On his return from the 1777 Danbury battle, General Washington praised Sybil for her heroism. But the public did not know of her courageous act until 1907, when her great-nephew, historian Louis S. Patrick, published an article about her extraordinary ride. In the years that followed, long poems about her heroic ride were published and her patriotic efforts were finally recognized. Historical markers now identify the route of her ride, and statues honoring her have been placed in New York, Connecticut, South Carolina, and Washington, D.C. In 1976, she was honored with a US postage stamp, part of a series recognizing mostly unknown contributors to the cause of the Revolutionary War.

Who Is Honorable?

Do you make promises to people? Maybe you told a friend that you would help him with homework. If you did help him, then you are honorable. You followed through on a promise. Think about people in your life who you respect—your teachers, your parents, your grandparents, your sports coach. Do you respect their opinions and what they teach you? If so, then you should honor them by listening to them. Tell them that you appreciate them.

Crazy Horse

Being honored by some but **vilified** by others is a common occurrence. The American government treated Crazy Horse, a Native American warrior, as a criminal for trying to protect the lands of his Lakota Sioux people. However, Crazy Horse's tribe honors him. Today, a monument honors him and the **heritage** of the Indians of North America.

Crazy Horse was born around 1843 near present-day Rapid City, South Dakota. By the time he was in his mid-teens, he was already an experienced warrior. He had fought in many battles against the white men **encroaching** on his native land. He fought against the US government again to defend his people's land after the Americans broke the 1868 Treaty of Fort Laramie. The treaty had been signed by General William T. Sherman

Crazy Horse was part of the Oglala Lakota tribe, which is one of the seven subtribes of the Lakota people.

and the Sioux people. It had promised: "As long as the rivers run and the grasses grow and trees bear leaves, Paha Sapa, the Black Hills, will forever and ever be the sacred land of the Indians." But around 1874, the treaty was violated when gold was found in the Black Hills. Soon, soldiers accompanied by miners and settlers moved into the territory.

Battling the US Army, unfortunately, became a way of life. On December 6, 1875, the US government declared that any Lakota Sioux not on a **reservation** must go to one that the US government had chosen for them. Crazy Horse and his 1,200 warriors refused, and they fought and defeated

Started in 1948, the Crazy Horse memorial will be the world's largest sculpture of a human head when it's finished, but as of 2017, it is far from completion.

General George Crook's troops at the Battle of Rosebud. They also later defeated General George Custer's **cavalry** at the Battle of Little Bighorn. Crazy Horse fought in many more battles during the American Indian Wars (1622 to 1924). He opposed life on a reservation or fleeing to Canada as others were doing.

Over time, the US soldiers killed thousands of Indians. In May 1877, Crazy Horse led his remaining followers to Fort Robinson to surrender. Though he had fought fearlessly to protect the ways of his people, the battle was lost. On September 5, 1877, while at the fort, he was wounded during a struggle and died when he attempted to leave the Pine Ridge Indian Reservation.

Started in 1948, a monument to Crazy Horse was carved into the mountains of the Black Hills of South Dakota. It depicts the Lakota warrior seated on his horse. The carving's pointed hand displays Crazy Horse's belief that his native land was wrongly taken by the US government. "My lands are where my dead lie buried," he had responded when asked scornfully by his captors, "Where are your lands now?" The memorial honors all Native Americans to commemorate their struggle.

The 14th Dalai Lama

Some people are honored just for being born. This is the case for the Dalai Lama, the spiritual leader of the Tibetan people. Tibetan Buddhists believe in **reincarnation**, and they identify the new Dalai Lama as the child who is the reincarnation of the previous Dalai Lama. Once found, the new Dalai Lama is revered and honored as the spiritual leader of the Tibetan people.

Lhamo Thondup was born on July 6, 1935, in Tibet. Search teams were sent throughout the region of Tibet to find the **incarnation** of the Dalai Lama. Following signs and visions, a team eventually found two-year-old Thondup. After a series of tests using the belongings of the previous Dalai Lama, the team identified him as the 14th Dalai Lama. At the age of four, he was formally recognized as the reincarnated Dalai, and he was

The 14th Dalai Lama cares about the environment and peaceful religious cooperation.

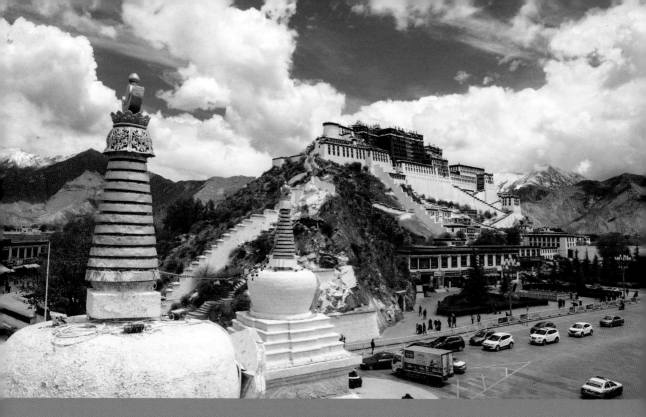

The 14th Dalai Lama grew up in the Potala Palace in Lhasa.

renamed Jetsun Jamphel Ngawang Lobsang Yeshe Tenzin Gyatso (Holy Lord, Gentle Glory, Compassionate, Defender of the Faith, Ocean of Wisdom). He was tutored in Buddhist philosophy and **enthroned** when he was 15 years old.

In 1951, China and its People's Liberation Army (PLA) occupied and ruled Tibet. In 1959, there was a Tibetan uprising against the foreign Chinese government. Ever since then, the 14th Dalai Lama has been in **exile** in India. Hundreds of thousands of Tibetan people followed him there. Then, he set up a government for the more than 80,000 refugees in the city of Dharamsala.

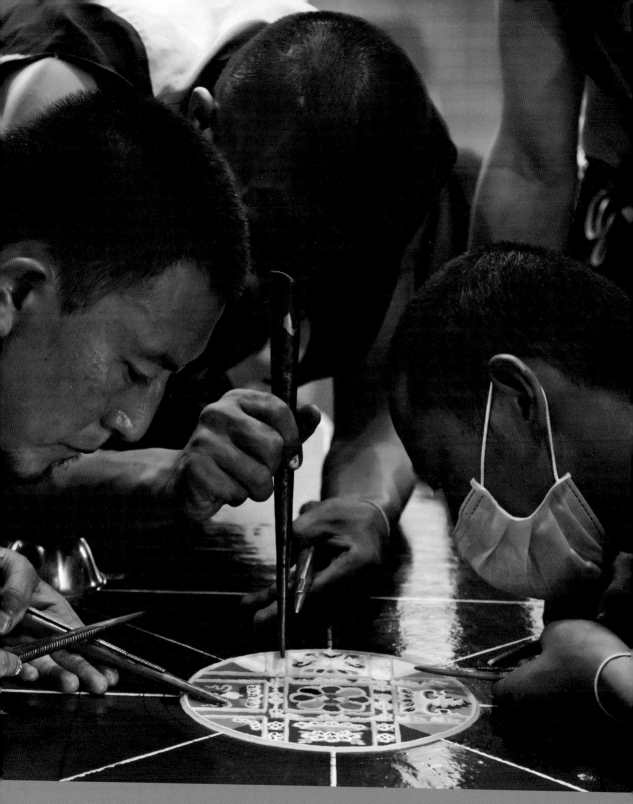
Tibetan monks make artwork from colored sand that is easily destroyed.

The Dalai Lama lives in a Tibetan temple in Dharamsala, India.

He also created an educational system in order to teach the children about the language, history, culture, and religion of the Tibetan people. Through his support of monasteries and nunneries, he has attempted to preserve Tibetan Buddhist teachings and the Tibetan way of life.

The 14th Dalai Lama is known as a man of peace for his commitment to the nonviolent struggle to **liberate** Tibet from Chinese rule. He has also traveled the world advocating for religious understanding and highlighting global environmental problems. He was awarded the 1989 Nobel Peace Prize for his work to create understanding and respect among the world's religions. He honors all people of the world and believes that we should all take responsibility for the world's needs. He said, "We must recognize that all beings want the same thing that we want. This is the way to achieve a true understanding."

It is unknown at this time whether a 15th Dalai Lama will follow. The 14th Dalai Lama has said that when he turns 90, he will set up a commission to determine if the institution should continue. If it will, then the process for finding his incarnation will also be decided. If a 15th Dalai Lama is recognized, that person will be honored as the new spiritual leader of Tibet.

Honor in the Workplace

Honor matters a lot in a career. Whether it's coworkers who have been working at your job longer than you or your boss, they have a lot of experience. These people can provide great advice if you listen to and respect them. You can be honorable, too. When you show others that they can rely on you, they will respect you and continue to take your opinions seriously. People like working with honorable people: they are trustworthy and cooperate well with others.

Wangari Maathai

Sometimes we honor people because of their work to honor the lives of others. Wangari Maathai dedicated her life to improving the lives of women and helping the environment. Her work to **reforest** land in her native country of Kenya helped to start a worldwide movement of community **empowerment**, a process where communities work to gain control over their lives. Her efforts contributed to the planting of more than 30 million trees to date.

Born April 1, 1940, in Kenya, Maathai was a well-known environmental activist and campaigner for human rights. She was also a teacher, and at the beginning of her career, she worked to establish equal benefits for the female staff at the

African forest elephants live in the Congo Basin, which is home to some of the world's largest tropical rainforests.

University of Nairobi. She was one of the first African women to receive a doctorate degree—the highest degree a college offers—and became the first female professor in Kenya. Through her involvement in a number of local organizations, she concluded that the cause of many of her community's problems was environmental **degradation**. To address this issue, she established the Green Belt Movement in Kenya. It worked to improve both local environments and the lives of women by paying them for planting trees in deforested areas.

Maathai was the first African woman to win the Nobel Prize.

Despite her accomplishments, the **authoritarian** Kenyan government opposed Maathai's pro-democratic and pro-women's rights views. At the time, women answered only to their husbands and did not complain publicly. Maathai served in the National Council of Women of Kenya and eventually became its chairman. She also helped women plant more than 20 million trees. The government accused her of treason and arrested her several times. Maathai said of the times, "It is often difficult to describe to those who live in a free society what life is like in an authoritarian regime. You don't know who to trust."

[21ST CENTURY SKILLS LIBRARY]

The government continued to develop forested land while Maathai's movement responded with peaceful protests and by planting trees.

Though her own government felt differently, the rest of the world honored Maathai for being a champion of women's rights and for her work with the Green Belt Movement. She was elected to the Kenyan parliament in 2002. The next year, she formed a new political party, the Mazingira Green Party of Kenya, making it possible for future candidates to run on a platform of environmental conservation. She was awarded the 2004 Nobel Peace Prize "for her contribution to sustainable development, democracy and peace." In 2009, the United Nations (UN) named Maathai a UN Messenger of Peace for her commitment to the environment and her desire to bring worldwide attention to the UN's work on climate change.

In 2011, Professor Wangari Maathai died of ovarian cancer. Today, her work is honored as a powerful example of **grassroots** organizing. And it's proof that one person's simple idea, like planting trees, can grow into a global environmental cause. The Green Belt Movement continues to fulfill Maathai's mission by reclaiming and reforesting Kenyan lands. It also has developed an empowering community for women.

Justice Sonia Sotomayor

People are sometimes honored for their position in their career field. Have you ever seen a video or television program about a court case? Sometimes a judge makes the final decision in a case. We refer to the judge as "Your Honor." In their field of work they are highly educated and respected. The highest court in the United States is the Supreme Court. Nine highly experienced judges make decisions about court cases that affect the way Americans live. Sonia Sotomayor is currently one of the judges on the Supreme Court.

Sotomayor was born in the Bronx on June 25, 1954, to Puerto Rican immigrant parents. Her father spoke little English, but her mother stressed the importance of an education and purchased a set of encyclopedias for Sonia to read and study.

Sotomayor is the 111th Justice of the Supreme Court.

Sotomayor's eighth grade graduation gown brings to mind her future as a judge in robes.

She decided at a young age that she wanted to be a judge after watching a popular TV legal drama called *Perry Mason*.

It takes many years of schooling and practice in the field of law to become a judge. After graduating **summa cum laude** from Princeton University in 1976, Sotomayor went on to law school at Yale University, getting her degree in 1979. While in school, she was a **social justice** activist, demanding fair treatment and representation of the Latino community. After passing the bar, she rose through the ranks as an assistant district attorney in New York. As a prosecutor, she was well known for her fairness. She was on many committees and boards while in New York, focusing on affordable housing, voting rights, and maternity care. Throughout her career, she worked for free for people and organizations that could not afford legal fees.

Sotomayor's first appointment as a judge was to the New York City district court in 1991. The next year, she was nominated by President George Bush and appointed to the US District Court. She became the first Hispanic federal judge in New York State. She earned a reputation as a fair but tough and well-prepared judge. President Bill Clinton nominated her for the US Court

Sotomayor and the other justices must respect the group's final decision.

of Appeals for the Second Circuit, and she served there for 10 years. In 2009, President Barack Obama nominated Sotomayor for a position in the US Supreme Court, and she was sworn in as an associate justice.

Since joining the court, she has been part of decisions on cases including health care, gay marriage, and **civil liberties**. As the court's first Latino judge and third female judge, she tends to have more liberal opinions, especially on cases regarding issues of race, gender, and ethnic identity.

Throughout her life, the Honorable Judge Sotomayor has shown concern for those disadvantaged because of race, income, and gender. Of her court opinions, she has said, "I strive never to forget the real-world consequences of my decisions on individuals, businesses, and government." She honors her duty to the court and the views of the other Supreme Court justices when she writes majority or **dissenting** opinions. And as a Supreme Court judge, she is honored for her experience in the **judicial** system and knowledge of the law.

What Have You Learned About Honor?

We show honor to others through respect and **gratitude**. *We can be honorable for following through on promises we make, accomplishing great deeds, or gaining knowledge and experience. The benefits of being honorable are that people know they can count on you and they respect you. Honor can be earned because of one action, because of a commitment to a group of people, or because of a lifetime of experience. People who are honorable can be trusted.*

Think About It

How Can You Become More Honorable?

You can become more honorable by following through on promises you make. You can also be a good citizen and do well in school. We are judged by our actions. Honorable people help others. Ask your parents what you can do to help people in your community. By helping others, you will earn their respect and be honored by them.

For More Information

Further Reading

Abbott, E. F. *Sybil Ludington: Revolutionary War Rider.* New York: Feiwel and Friends, 2017.

Barrington, Richard. *Sonia Sotomayor: The Supreme Court's First Hispanic Justice.* New York: Britannica Educational Publishing, 2015.

UNESCO. *Wangari Maathai and the Green Belt Movement.* London: HarperCollins, 2015.

Websites

Crazy Horse Memorial—The Crazy Horse Memorial Story
https://crazyhorsememorial.org/the-crazy-horse-memorial-story.html
Learn more about Crazy Horse and his memorial in South Dakota.

The Green Belt Movement—Who We Are
www.greenbeltmovement.org/who-we-are
Check out the official website of the Green Belt Movement highlighting its founder, mission, and projects.

Nobel Prize—The 14th Dalai Lama
www.nobelprize.org/nobel_prizes/peace/laureates/1989/lama-bio.html
Visit the official Nobel Prize website for information, videos, photos, and speeches highlighting the 14th Dalai Lama's life and actions.

GLOSSARY

authoritarian (uh-thor-ih-TAIR-ee-uhn) not allowing personal freedom through restrictive laws

cavalry (KAV-uhl-ree) the part of an army that rides horses

civil liberties (SIV-uhl LIB-ur-teez) the rights granted to people to speak, think, gather, organize, and worship freely

degradation (deg-ruh-DAY-shuhn) the process of damaging or ruining something

dissenting (di-SENT-ing) disagreeing with an official decision

empowerment (em-POU-er-ment) power given to someone to do something

encroaching (en-KROHCH-ing) gradually moving into an area that is beyond the established limits

enthroned (en-THROHND) to be made a ruler in a formal ceremony

exile (EG-zile) a situation in which you are forced to leave your country or home and live in a foreign country

grassroots (GRAS-roots) operated by ordinary people in a society and not political leaders

gratitude (GRAT-ih-tood) a feeling of being grateful or thankful

heritage (HER-ih-tij) traditions and beliefs that a group considers an important part of its history

incarnation (in-kar-NAY-shuhn) one of a series of lives that a person is believed to have had

judicial (joo-DISH-uhl) relating to courts of law or judges

liberate (LIB-uh-rate) to free something from being controlled by another government

militia (muh-LISH-uh) a group of people who are not part of the armed forces of a country but are trained as soldiers

reforest (ree-FOR-est) to replant trees where all the original trees were cut down or destroyed by disaster

regiment (REJ-uh-muhnt) a large military unit that is usually made up of several large groups of soldiers

reincarnation (ree-in-kahr-NAY-shuhn) being born again in another body after dying

reservation (rez-ur-VAY-shuhn) an area of land in the United States that is kept separate as a place for Native Americans to live

social justice (SOH-shuhl JUST-tis) the view that everyone deserves equal economic, political, and social opportunities

summa cum laude (SOOM-uh KOOM LAH-dey) with highest honor or achievement

vilified (VIL-ih-fyed) to have unpleasant things said or written about someone in order to cause other people to have a bad opinion of that person

INDEX